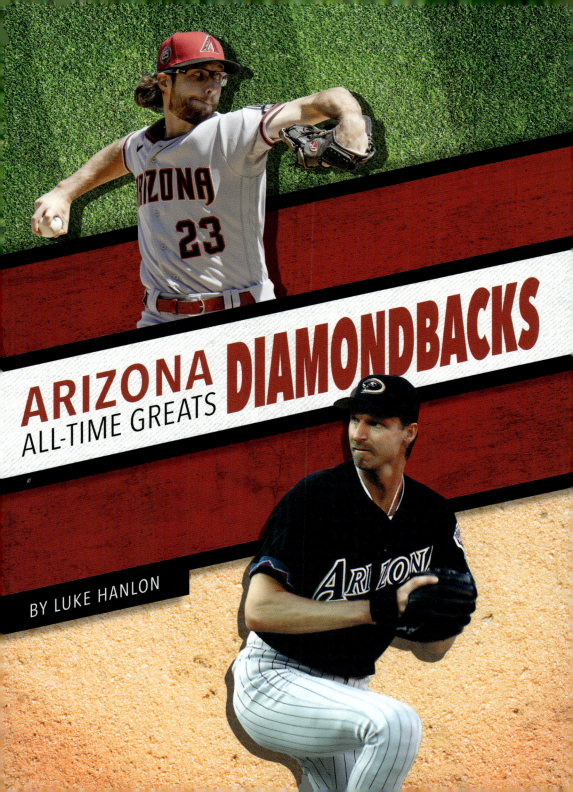

ARIZONA DIAMONDBACKS
ALL-TIME GREATS

BY LUKE HANLON

Copyright © 2024 by Press Room Editions. All rights reserved. No part of this book may be used or reproduced in any manner whatsoever, including internet usage, without written permission from the copyright owner, except in the case of brief quotations embodied in critical articles and reviews.

Book design by Jake Slavik
Cover design by Jake Slavik

Photographs ©: Gregory Bull/AP Images, cover (top), 1 (top); Tom DiPace/AP Images, cover (bottom), 1 (bottom); Brian Bahr/Getty Images Sport/Getty Images, 4, 7; Jeff Gross/Allsport/Getty Images Sport/Getty Images, 8; Christian Petersen/Getty Images Sport/Getty Images, 10, 19; Scott Cunningham/Getty Images Sport/Getty Images, 13, 16; Denis Poroy/Getty Images Sport/Getty Images, 14; Norm Hall/Getty Images Sport/Getty Images, 20

Press Box Books, an imprint of Press Room Editions.

ISBN
978-1-63494-792-3 (library bound)
978-1-63494-812-8 (paperback)
978-1-63494-850-0 (epub)
978-1-63494-832-6 (hosted ebook)

Library of Congress Control Number: 2023909963

Distributed by North Star Editions, Inc.
2297 Waters Drive
Mendota Heights, MN 55120
www.northstareditions.com

Printed in the United States of America
012024

ABOUT THE AUTHOR

Luke Hanlon is a sportswriter and editor based in Minneapolis.

TABLE OF CONTENTS

CHAPTER 1
QUICK SUCCESS 5

CHAPTER 2
HEATING UP 11

CHAPTER 3
SNAKEBIT 17

TIMELINE 22
TEAM FACTS 23
MORE INFORMATION 23
GLOSSARY 24
INDEX 24

CHAPTER 1
QUICK SUCCESS

The Arizona Diamondbacks became a Major League Baseball (MLB) team in 1998. Despite being an expansion team, the Diamondbacks found early success. In their second season, they won 100 games and made the playoffs.

Matt Williams was one reason why. The third baseman had a lot of pop in his bat. His 142 runs batted in (RBIs) led the team in 1999. Batting directly before Williams in the lineup was **Luis Gonzalez**. The left fielder led the National League (NL) in hits in 1999. Always a fan favorite, Gonzalez made five All-Star teams with Arizona.

Steve Finley was another staple of the Arizona lineup thanks to his mixture of speed and power. While Finley consistently hit home runs for the Diamondbacks, his defense in center field was his biggest strength. He won Gold Gloves in 1999 and 2000. That award is given to the best defensive player at each position.

The Diamondbacks had a star pitching rotation to match their powerful lineup. **Randy Johnson** signed with Arizona before the 1999

STAT SPOTLIGHT

CAREER STRIKEOUTS
DIAMONDBACKS TEAM RECORD
Randy Johnson: 2,077

season. The "Big Unit" was already one of the league's best pitchers. Standing 6-foot-10 (208 cm), the towering lefty overpowered hitters with his velocity. Starting in 1999, Johnson won the Cy Young Award four years in a row. That honor is given to the best pitcher in each league. Johnson recorded at least 334 strikeouts in each season, leading the league each time.

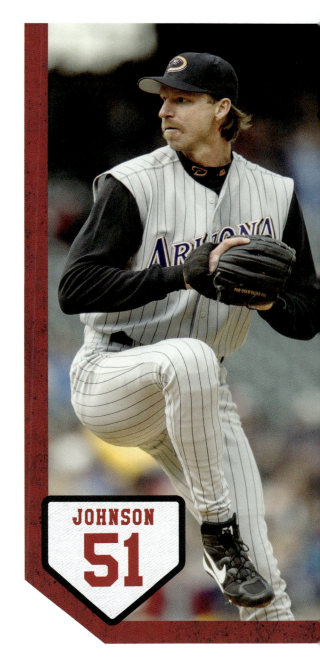

In 2000, the Diamondbacks traded for **Curt Schilling**. Like Johnson, Schilling had a dangerous fastball. And he rarely walked opposing batters.

This core led the upstart Diamondbacks to the 2001 World Series. The duo of Johnson and Schilling was a force against the New York Yankees. The epic series went to Game 7 in Arizona. Schilling started in front of his home fans at Bank One Ballpark. And Johnson came out of the bullpen to limit the Yankees lineup to two runs. With the game tied in the bottom of the ninth, Gonzalez came to the plate with the bases loaded. He hit a bloop single over the shortstop's head to win the World Series for the Diamondbacks.

GREATNESS TOGETHER

Randy Johnson and Curt Schilling were named co-Most Valuable Player (MVP) of the 2001 World Series. It was only the second time that happened. The duo led the Diamondbacks to the fastest World Series win for an expansion team in MLB history.

CHAPTER 2
HEATING UP

The core of the World Series team quickly disbanded. With Schilling gone halfway through the 2003 season and Johnson aging, the Diamondbacks found a new ace to build their pitching staff around. **Brandon Webb** had a strong rookie year, recording a career-best 2.84 earned-run average (ERA). By 2006, the righty was one of the best pitchers in baseball. Webb pitched three shutouts that season and earned the NL Cy Young Award.

Two young outfielders thrived in 2007 and provided some run support for Webb. Center fielder **Chris Young** smashed a career-high

32 home runs as a rookie in 2007. The speedster also stole 27 bases. He was the first rookie in MLB history to hit more than 30 home runs and steal more than 25 bases.

Joining Young in the outfield was 19-year-old **Justin Upton**. Like Young, Upton had power and speed. He added range in the outfield as well, making him a complete player. Those skills led to Upton playing in two All-Star Games with Arizona.

The Diamondbacks traded for starting pitcher **Dan Haren** in 2008 to bolster

UNUSUAL HISTORY
On June 25, 2010, Edwin Jackson completed the second no-hitter in Diamondbacks history. But it was far from an easy night. Jackson walked eight Tampa Bay Rays batters and hit another on his way to throwing 149 pitches.

their rotation. He didn't throw very hard. But his excellent control kept hitters off-balance. Haren was an All-Star in both of his full seasons with Arizona.

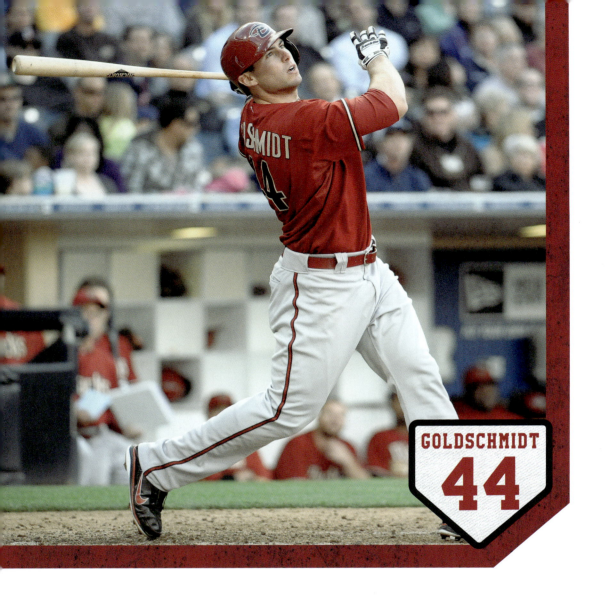

In 2010, the Diamondbacks only won 65 games. It seemed like a long rebuild was on the way. However, the core of Young, Upton, and rookie **Paul Goldschmidt** lifted the

Diamondbacks to first place in the NL West the very next season. By 2013, Goldschmidt was in the NL MVP conversation almost every season. The first baseman was a complete hitter. In three separate seasons, he hit more than 30 home runs and recorded more than 100 RBIs.

While Goldschmidt was terrorizing opposing pitchers, center fielder **AJ Pollock** was frustrating opposing batters with his defense. Pollock rarely made an error. He was rewarded for that in 2015, earning a Gold Glove and an All-Star appearance.

STAT SPOTLIGHT

WALKS IN A SEASON
DIAMONDBACKS TEAM RECORD
Paul Goldschmidt: 118 (2015)

CHAPTER 3
SNAKEBIT

Once the Diamondbacks knew they had a star in Paul Goldschmidt, they worked on building a team around him. One new arrival was **David Peralta**. Arizona called him up from the minors in 2014. The left fielder was consistent at the plate and in the field. "Freight Train" led the NL in triples in 2015 and 2021. He also won a Gold Glove in 2019.

> **STAT SPOTLIGHT**
>
> **DOUBLES IN A GAME**
> DIAMONDBACKS TEAM RECORD
> **David Peralta: 4** (April 22, 2017)

In 2016, the Diamondbacks made one of their biggest moves yet when they signed **Zack Greinke**. The righty pitcher had won the AL Cy Young Award with the Kansas City Royals and was a three-time All-Star. In just four seasons with Arizona, he matched that number of All-Star appearances. Greinke had elite control and a devastating changeup that fooled hitters. His defense was also strong. Greinke won four Gold Glove Awards with the Diamondbacks.

In the rotation along with Greinke was **Robbie Ray**. It took some time for the lefty to develop. But he blossomed

POWER PITCHER

Until 2022, pitchers in the NL also had to bat in the lineup. Most pitchers were easy outs or tried to lay down sacrifice bunts. Not Zack Greinke, though. In 48 at bats for Arizona in 2019, Greinke hit three home runs and racked up eight RBIs.

in 2017, making the All-Star Game with a 2.89 ERA. Ray's breaking pitches helped him strike out more than 200 batters in three separate seasons with Arizona.

The Diamondbacks found two new hitters to bolster their lineup in the late 2010s. In 2016, they traded for **Ketel Marte**. He used his versatility to play all over the field. And he was

strong at the plate. Marte hit new heights in 2019 when he had a .329 batting average and blasted 32 home runs.

That same year, **Christian Walker** became a regular in Arizona's lineup. The first baseman had to sit behind Goldschmidt for two years. But he made the most of his playing time once the Diamondbacks traded Goldschmidt after the 2018 season. Walker was at his best in 2022, hitting a career-high 36 home runs while winning a Gold Glove.

Heading into the 2020s, the Diamondbacks found another ace in **Zac Gallen**. The "Milkman" registered an ERA lower than 3.00 in three of his first four seasons with Arizona. Marte, Walker, and Gallen gave Arizona fans hope that another deep playoff run was on the horizon.

TIMELINE

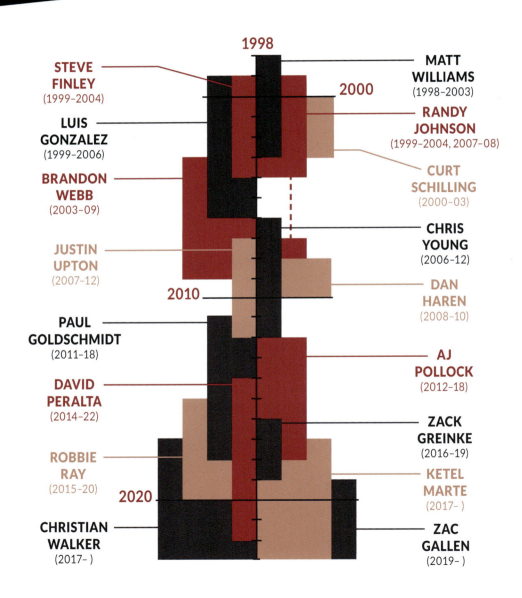

TEAM FACTS

ARIZONA DIAMONDBACKS

Founded: 1998

World Series titles: 1 (2001)*

Key managers:

   Bob Brenly (2001-04)

      303-262 (.536), 1 World Series title

   Buck Showalter (1998-2000)

      250-236 (.514)

MORE INFORMATION

To learn more about the Arizona Diamondbacks, go to **pressboxbooks.com/AllAccess**.

These links are routinely monitored and updated to provide the most current information available.

*through 2022

GLOSSARY

ace
The best starting pitcher on a team.

elite
The best of the best.

error
When a fielder fails to make what is considered a routine play.

expansion team
A new team added to an established professional sports league.

no-hitter
A game in which a pitcher, or combination of pitchers, doesn't allow any hits.

rookie
A first-year player.

shutout
When a pitcher doesn't allow a run.

upstart
A person or group that has quickly risen to a position of power.

velocity
The maximum speed of a pitch.

INDEX

Finley, Steve, 6

Gallen, Zac, 21
Goldschmidt, Paul, 14–15, 17, 21
Gonzalez, Luis, 5–6, 9
Greinke Zach, 18

Haren, Dan, 12–13

Jackson, Edwin, 12

Johnson, Randy, 6–9, 11

Marte, Ketel, 19, 21

Peralta, David, 17
Pollock, AJ, 15

Ray, Robbie, 18–19

Schilling, Curt, 8–9, 11

Upton, Justin, 12, 14

Walker, Christian, 21
Webb, Brandon, 11
Williams, Matt, 5

Young, Chris, 11–12, 14